KIDMEN:
A MANIFESTO FOR
MEN SERVING IN CHILDREN'S MINISTRY

RYAN FRANK

PUBLISHING

Cover design by Andrew Brooks - andrewbrooks.crtv@gmail.com
Interior layout by Nicole Jones - kneecoalgrace@gmail.com
Edited by Theda Crawford- thedacrawford4133@gmail.com

ISBN: 9781088111390
ISBN (ebook): 9781088111475

To my father-in-law Terry, whose 36-year faithful pastorate at the same church began in children's ministry, an inspiration and guiding light in my own journey as a children's ministry leader.

GEORGE BARNA

"In the race to a child's heart, the first one there wins."

D.L. MOODY

"If I could relive my life,
I would devote it entirely to reaching children for God."

INTRODUCTION

Thank you for choosing to pick up this book, KidMEN: A Manifesto for Men in Children's Ministry. As someone who has dedicated his life to serving children and families in the church, I know firsthand how important it is to have resources and guidance to navigate the challenges and opportunities that come with this calling. That is why I am excited to share this book with you.

My journey in vocational children's ministry began during college. I felt a calling to serve in this ministry, and I quickly realized how much I enjoyed working with kids and families. However, I also noticed this: there were few men serving in children's ministry. This troubled me because I knew the impact that positive male role models could have on children's lives.

Over the years, I have seen the value and impact that men can have in children's ministry. They bring unique perspectives and strengths to the role, and their presence can make a difference in the lives of both boys and girls. However, I also know that serving in children's ministry as a man can come with its own set of challenges.

That is why I wrote this book. KidMEN is a manifesto for men serving in children's ministry, filled with practical advice, encouragement, and wisdom for navigating the challenges and opportunities that come with it. Whether you are just starting out in children's ministry or you have been serving for years, this book is for you.

We will cover a lot of ground in this little book. We will explore the importance of children's ministry and specifically the role that men can play in this area. We will examine some of the challenges and opportunities that exist for men who serve in children's ministry and discuss how to overcome those challenges and make the most of those opportunities.

We will also dive into the practical aspects of serving in children's ministry. We will discuss how to recruit and train volunteers, create engaging and impactful programs, and develop meaningful relationships with kids and families.

We will also focus on personal growth and development as a leader in children's ministry. We will discuss how to manage time and balance responsibilities, how to develop and maintain healthy relationships with other staff members and volunteers, and how to navigate conflicts and challenges that may arise. We will explore things like how to develop as a mentor and how to ensure that your own spiritual and emotional needs are being met.

I am honored to share my knowledge and experience with you through this book. It is my hope that KidMEN will be a valuable resource and encouragement to you as you continue on your journey in children's ministry. Thank you for your dedication to serving children and families in the church, and I pray that this book will help you to grow and thrive in your important role.

IT'S A GIRLS JOB

For many years, the role of children's ministry leader has been associated with women. This has been the mindset despite the fact that there are many men – like you and me – who have a passion for working with children and families in the church.

While it is true that the majority of children's ministry leaders are women, this does not mean that it is a job exclusively for women. In fact, men can bring unique perspectives and strengths to the role, and their presence can be a positive influence for children of all genders. Men can actually make great children's ministry leaders in the church and there are several benefits, also.

First, kids need positive male role models. Many kids may not have positive male role models in their lives. Men in children's ministry can provide a positive influence for these kids, showing them what it means to be a caring, responsible, and compassionate man.

Second, it's a strengths-based approach. Men and women tend to have different strengths, and these strengths can be beneficial in a children's ministry setting. A diverse team of leaders, including both men and women, can create a well-rounded program that meets the needs of the church. Having a mix of men and women leading children's ministry can provide children with diverse role models and perspectives.

Third, it encourages other men to get involved. I see it all the time. When men are involved in children's ministry leadership, other men are more apt to get involved themselves.

Sure, a majority of children's ministry leaders may be women and I am thankful for each one of them. But hear me on this. Men have just as much to offer in this important role! It is time to break down the misconception that children's ministry leadership is a job exclusively for the girls and encourage men to get involved and make a difference in the lives of children and families in the church.

THE CHURCH OF THE CHILDREN.

D.L. Moody, one of the most influential Christian leaders of the 19th century, had a heart for children in downtown Chicago. Moody was a man of great faith who dedicated his life to sharing the Gospel with people of all ages, and his work with children is a testament to his passion for reaching the next generation.

Moody grew up in poverty in Northfield, Massachusetts, and had little formal education. Despite this, he became a successful businessman in Chicago in the mid-1800's. However, his life was transformed when he accepted Jesus Christ as his Savior at the age of 18. He became deeply committed to sharing the Gospel and soon began to feel called to work with children.

In 1860, Moody began holding Sunday School classes in the poor neighborhoods of Chicago. These classes were a lifeline for many children, who often came from broken homes and difficult circumstances. Moody's approach to teaching was simple but effective. He used stories and illustrations to make the Bible come alive for the children, and he showed them love and compassion, regardless of their background or social status.

Moody's work with children grew rapidly, and he soon founded the Illinois Street Church, which became known as the "church of the children." He also founded the Moody Church, which remains a prominent church in Chicago to this day. His work with children continued throughout his life, and he is perhaps best known for founding the Northfield School for Girls and the Mount Hermon School for Boys.

Moody is credited with saying, "If I could relive my life, I would devote it entirely to reaching children for God."

Moody's heart for children in downtown Chicago is a powerful example for men who are leading children's ministries in churches today. Like Moody, these men have a unique opportunity to make a difference in the lives of children, many of whom may come from difficult backgrounds or face challenging circumstances.

WHEN ARE YOU GOING TO BE THE YOUTH PASTOR?

As a man serving in children's ministry, it's likely that you've encountered the stereotypes and misconceptions that come with this role. Perhaps you've been asked when you're going to move on to a "real" ministry like youth ministry or even become a lead pastor. These questions can be discouraging, but it's important not to let them get the best of you.

The truth is, children's ministry is a real and important ministry in its own right. It's not a stepping stone or a lesser ministry, but a calling that requires skill, dedication, and a heart for God's youngest children. You have been called to this ministry for a reason, and it's important not to compare yourself to others or let others' opinions distract you from your calling.

It's easy to get caught up in the opinions of others and start to doubt our own calling. But we must remember that our calling comes from God, not from man. It's not about what others think we should be doing or where they think we should be going, but about what God has called us to do in this season of our lives.

Remember that comparisons are not helpful. God has uniquely gifted and called each of us for a specific purpose. It's not productive to compare ourselves to others, as we each have our own God-ordained paths to follow. We should focus on living out our own calling, rather than trying to fit into someone else's mold or measure up to someone else's expectations.

Furthermore, we must recognize that the questions and stereotypes we face may be tools of the enemy to distract and discourage us from our calling. Satan would love nothing more than for us to doubt our calling and give up on the ministry that God has entrusted to us. But we must remember that we are in a battle, and we must put on the armor of God and stand firm in our calling.

So, how can we stay focused on our calling and not let the stereotypes and questions of others get the best of us? Here are a few practical tips.

It starts by surrounding yourself with a supportive community. Find other men who are serving in children's ministry or other similar ministries, and build relationships with them. Encourage one another and remind each other of the importance of your work.

Stay grounded in God's Word. Spend time in prayer and study of the Bible, so that you can be reminded of your identity in Christ and the calling that He has placed on your life.

Seek feedback and support from the leadership in your church. Talk to your pastor or other church leaders about your ministry and your calling, and seek their input and guidance. They may be able to offer helpful advice or encouragement.

Remember the impact you are making. Think about the children and families whose lives you are touching through your ministry. Remember that your work is making a difference, even if it's not always visible or acknowledged by others.

Don't let the stereotypes and opinions of others distract you from your calling in children's ministry. Remember that this is a real and important ministry and that you have been called to it for a reason. Don't compare yourself to others, but focus on living out your own calling and trusting in God's plan for your life.

KEEP YOUR EYES ON JESUS.

Beth and I visited the Holy Land in Israel recently and took a boat ride on the Sea of Galilee where Peter walked on the water. Do you remember the story? It's a powerful reminder to ministry leaders that joy comes from keeping our eyes on Jesus, not people. People will let you down, but Jesus will never let you down. Peter saw Jesus walking on water and asked to join Him. Jesus invited Peter to step out of the boat and walk on water towards Him. At first, Peter succeeded, but he began to sink when he focused on the wind and waves instead of Jesus.

Even in the midst of challenges and pressures, when we trust in Jesus' power and love; we can experience joy and fulfillment in our ministry. Don't get your eyes on the people or the problems. Like Peter, keep your eyes fixed on Jesus! Remember the words of Psalm 16:8: "I keep my eyes always on the Lord. With Him at my right hand, I will not be shaken."

YOU ARE CALLED.

Being called by God into ministry is a profound and life-changing experience. It means that God has chosen you for a specific purpose and has equipped you with the skills and gifts necessary to fulfill that purpose. It's a calling that requires faith, obedience, and humility.

If you are a man who has been called into children's ministry, it's important to embrace that calling and follow where God is leading you. This can be a scary and uncertain journey, but it's important to trust in God's plan for your life and step out in faith.

Embracing your calling may mean making sacrifices, such as leaving a comfortable job or relocating to a new city. It may mean facing opposition or criticism from others who don't understand your calling. But it also means experiencing the joy and fulfillment of serving God and making a difference in the lives of kids and their families.

To embrace your calling, it's important to seek God's guidance and direction. Spend time in prayer and study of the Bible, and listen for the still small voice of the Holy Spirit. Seek the counsel of wise and trusted mentors, and surround yourself with a supportive community of fellow believers.

It's also important to cultivate a heart of humility and service. Remember that ministry is not about building your own kingdom or gaining recognition for yourself, but about serving God and others. Look for opportunities to serve and love those around you, whether it's through your ministry or in everyday life.

Above all, remember that your calling is a gift from God. It's not something that you have earned or deserved, but something that God has graciously given to you. Embrace your calling with gratitude and humility, and trust in God's faithfulness to guide you every step of the way.

PASSING ON FAITH FROM ONE GENERATION TO THE NEXT.

The Bible provides a strong foundation for ministry to kids and families in the church. From the very beginning, God has demonstrated his love for children and his desire for them to be included in his kingdom.

One of the most well-known passages about children is found in Matthew 19:13-15, where parents brought their children to Jesus to be blessed. The disciples rebuked the parents for bothering Jesus, but He responded by saying, "Let the little children come to Me and do not hinder them, for to such belongs the kingdom of heaven."

This passage not only demonstrates Jesus' love and acceptance of children, but also highlights the importance of including them in the kingdom of God. As those who follow Jesus, we are called to welcome children into our churches and to help them grow in their faith.

Another important biblical basis for ministry to kids and families is found in Deuteronomy 6:4-9. This passage, known as the Shema, instructs God's people to love Him with all their heart, soul, and strength, and to teach his commandments to their children. It emphasizes the importance of passing on faith from one generation to the next.

The apostle Paul also provides insight into ministry to families in his letter to the Ephesians. In Ephesians 6:1-4, Paul instructs children to obey their parents and parents to raise their children in the training and instruction of the Lord. He also reminds fathers not to exasperate their children, but to bring them up in the nurture and admonition of the Lord.

These passages and others like them demonstrate the biblical basis for ministry to kids and families in the church. They show us that children are not just the future of the church, but an important part of it now. They also demonstrate God's desire for families to be united in faith and for parents to take an active role in the spiritual growth of their children.

As those who minister to children and families, we have the privilege and responsibility of helping them grow in their faith and love for Jesus. This includes providing opportunities for them to learn about God's love and grace, as well as creating a welcoming and inclusive community where they can belong and grow.

DEALING WITH DIFFICULT PEOPLE.

Dealing with difficult people in ministry can be a challenging aspect of leadership, whether it involves a staff member, a parent, or a volunteer. However, it is crucial to approach these situations with wisdom, grace, and a servant's heart. Here are some principles to consider when navigating these difficult relationships.

First and foremost, seek to understand and empathize with the person's perspective. Often, difficult behaviors stem from underlying concerns, misunderstandings, or personal struggles. Take the time to actively listen, allowing them to express their thoughts and emotions. By seeking understanding, you demonstrate your care and respect for their feelings, which can help diffuse tension and pave the way for meaningful dialogue.

Second, practice forgiveness and extend grace. Holding onto grudges or responding with anger will only exacerbate difficult situations. Instead, choose to forgive and extend grace as Christ has forgiven and shown grace to us. Remember Ephesians 4:32 says, "Be kind and compassionate to one another, forgiving each other, just as in Christ God forgave you." Allow the love and mercy of Christ to guide your responses and interactions.

Third, engage in open and honest communication. Address concerns or conflicts directly, seeking resolution in a respectful and constructive manner. Choose words and tones that promote understanding and reconciliation. Proverbs 15:1 reminds us that "A gentle answer turns away wrath, but a harsh word stirs up anger." Cultivate an environment where difficult conversations can take place with respect and love.

Finally, seek guidance and support from mentors, leaders, or pastoral staff. Talk with people who can provide wisdom and counsel in navigating sticky and difficult conversations. They can offer perspective, advice, and prayer support to help you handle challenging situations in a godly manner.

Dealing with difficult people in ministry requires patience, wisdom, and a Christ-like attitude. Seek to understand, set healthy boundaries, practice forgiveness, engage in open communication, and seek guidance when needed. Remember the words of Romans 12:18: "If it is possible, as far as it depends on you, live at peace with everyone." Trust in God's guidance and rely on his grace as you navigate these challenging relationships, seeking to bring unity, reconciliation, and growth in the ministry for his glory.

WHAT EVERY KID NEEDS.

You have a unique opportunity to impact the lives of the children in your care. While each child is unique and has his/her own set of needs, there are certain things that every child needs from you as a children's ministry leader.

First and foremost, children need to feel loved and accepted. They need to know that they are valued and appreciated for who they are, regardless of their background or abilities.

Children also need a safe and welcoming environment. They need a place where they can feel comfortable being themselves, without fear of judgment or rejection.

Another important thing that children need from a children's ministry leader is guidance and direction. Children are still learning and growing, and they need adults who can help them navigate the challenges of life.

Children also need consistency and dependability from their children's ministry leaders. They need to know that they can count on their leader to show up each week, to be present and engaged, and to provide a stable presence in their lives.

In addition, children need encouragement and affirmation. They need to know that they are capable of achieving great things and that God has an amazing destiny for their lives.

To sum it up, every child needs to feel loved and accepted, a safe and welcoming environment, guidance and direction, consistency and dependability, and encouragement and affirmation. Children's ministry leaders – like you – who provide these things are making a positive impact on the lives of the kids in their care and helping them fulfill their God-given destinies.

GENDER BALANCE IN KIDMIN.

Having a gender-balanced team is crucial for a healthy and effective children's ministry. Both men and women bring unique gifts and perspectives to the table, and a team that is all male or all female misses out on the benefits of diversity.

Having male volunteers in children's ministry is particularly important. It provides positive male role models for children who may not have them at home, and helps boys develop a sense of identity and purpose as they see men actively engaged in serving and caring for children.

At the same time, it's important not to view men in children's ministry solely as role models for boys. They are equally valuable in ministering to girls and families, providing a balance of perspectives and experiences that helps create a well-rounded ministry.

Women also bring unique gifts and perspectives to children's ministry, and should be valued as much as men. However, when women are over-represented in volunteer positions, it can create an unintentional message that men are not as capable or interested in serving in these roles.

Having a gender-balanced team also helps ensure that both boys and girls receive equal attention and care from volunteers. Boys may be more likely to connect with male volunteers, while girls may prefer female volunteers, and having a mix of both helps ensure that all children feel seen and valued.

Finally, having a gender-balanced team helps guard against potential issues related to inappropriate behavior or accusations of misconduct. While the vast majority of volunteers have pure motives and good intentions, having both male and female volunteers helps ensure that there is accountability and transparency in all interactions with children.

In short, a gender-balanced team is essential for a healthy and effective children's ministry. Both men and women bring unique gifts and perspectives to the table, and by working together, they can create a ministry that is welcoming, nurturing, and life-changing for all children and families involved.

A HEART FOR THE MOST VULNERABLE AND MARGINALIZED.

Bill Wilson is a remarkable man who has made a huge impact in the lives of children and families in New York City. Born and raised in Brooklyn, Wilson had a difficult childhood marked by poverty and abuse. As a result, he had a deep empathy for children who were facing similar struggles.

In 1989, Wilson founded Metro World Child, a ministry dedicated to reaching and serving the children of New York City. He started out with just a few volunteers, but the ministry quickly grew as more and more people saw the impact it was having on the lives of children.

One of the unique things about Metro World Child is its focus on bringing the Gospel to children right where they are. Wilson and his team go into the most impoverished and dangerous neighborhoods in the city, setting up tents and conducting sidewalk Sunday Schools. They also have mobile ministry units that go into housing projects, homeless shelters, and other areas where children are in need.

Over the years, Metro World Child has grown to become one of the largest Sunday School programs in the world, with over 100,000 children participating each week. The ministry also provides other services such as after-school programs, mentoring, and summer camps.

What's most inspiring about Bill Wilson is his unwavering commitment to serving the children of New York City, even in the face of tremendous obstacles. He has faced opposition from gangs, drug dealers, and even city officials who have tried to shut down his ministry. But he has persisted, believing that every child is worth fighting for.

Men serving in kid's ministry can learn a lot from Bill Wilson's example. He shows us that ministry is messy and often uncomfortable, but it's worth it to see lives transformed by the Gospel. He also shows us the importance of having a heart for the most vulnerable and marginalized children in our communities. By following his lead, men serving in kid's ministry can make a real difference in the lives of children and families, just like him.

BALANCING WORK AND HOME.

One of the biggest challenges in ministry is balancing the demands of ministry with the responsibilities of home and family. It's not easy to juggle the needs of your church with the needs of your spouse and children, but it's essential to find a healthy balance that works for you.

One of the keys to balancing work and home is setting clear boundaries. This means knowing when to say no to certain ministry responsibilities or events that would take time away from your family. It also means being intentional about carving out time for your spouse and children, whether that's regular date nights with your wife or dedicated time for family activities.

It's important to remember that your family should always come first, even if that means stepping back from ministry for a season. Your role as a husband and father is more important than your role as a kid's ministry leader. When you prioritize your family, you'll find that your ministry becomes more effective because you're coming from a place of strength and stability.

Another important aspect of balancing work and home is communication. It's crucial to have open and honest communication with your spouse about your ministry responsibilities and the impact they're having on your family. This means being willing to listen to your spouse's concerns and making adjustments as needed. On several occasions, Beth has said, "Ryan, put your phone down" during times I have been too preoccupied with work at home.

Take time to communicate with your ministry team about your family commitments and the need for flexibility. A good team will understand the importance of family and will work with you to find a balance that works for everyone.

It's also important to take care of yourself. When you're constantly juggling the demands of ministry and family, it's easy to neglect your own needs. But taking care of yourself physically, emotionally, and spiritually is essential if you want to be effective in both areas of your life. This might mean taking time for exercise, hobbies, or other activities that recharge your batteries.

Finally, it's essential to stay connected to God through prayer and Bible study. When you're grounded in your faith, you'll have the strength and wisdom to navigate the challenges of balancing work and home. You'll also be able to hear from God about the specific ways He wants you to serve in ministry and how to prioritize your family.

Balancing work and home is one of the biggest challenges facing leaders in kid's ministry. But it's essential to find a healthy balance that works for you and your family. By setting clear boundaries, communicating with your spouse and ministry team, taking care of yourself, and staying connected to God; you can thrive both in ministry and at home. Remember, your family is your first ministry and when you prioritize them, your ministry will become even more effective.

CONNECTING WITH FAMILIES DURING THE WEEK.

Connecting with families outside of Sunday services is essential for effective children's ministry. As a kid's pastor, it's important to build relationships with parents and grandparents, understand their needs, and provide support and resources for them.

This can be done a million different ways. Try hosting family events, sending out emails, engaging on social media, making phone calls or home visits, and providing resources like parenting classes or support groups. When families feel connected and supported, they are more likely to stay engaged and committed to the church community.

In addition, connecting with families outside of Sunday services allows for opportunities to share the Gospel and disciple families in their faith journey. By building relationships with families and earning their trust, you can help facilitate spiritual growth and transformation in both children and parents.

EAT THE FROG FIRST.

Staying productive is a crucial aspect of effective leadership, especially in the demanding role of children's ministry. One valuable principle for boosting productivity is the concept of "eating the frog first." I wrote a book with this title a few years back. This principle encourages you to tackle the most difficult and undesirable tasks early in the day. By prioritizing these challenging tasks, you set the tone for increased productivity and momentum throughout your work.

The essence of eating the frog first lies in confronting tasks that require the most effort, concentration, or creativity which might be easily postponed or avoided. It's tempting to procrastinate on these tasks, but doing so often leads to diminished productivity and a constant sense of unfinished business. By taking proactive steps to address these challenging tasks head-on, you create a sense of accomplishment, gain a surge of momentum, and free up mental space for other important activities.

To embrace the principle of eating the frog first, consider implementing these tips for productivity:

1. Identify your frogs: Take time to assess your tasks and determine which ones are the most challenging or time-consuming. These are the frogs that should be at the top of your priority list.

2. Set clear goals and deadlines: Break down your tasks into specific goals and set realistic deadlines. Having a clear roadmap helps you stay focused and motivated.

3. Eliminate distractions: Minimize distractions that can derail your productivity. Turn off notifications on your phone, close unnecessary tabs on your computer, and create a conducive environment for focused work.

4. Use time-blocking: Allocate dedicated time blocks for specific tasks, including eating the frog. This practice ensures that important tasks receive the attention they deserve and prevents them from being pushed aside.

5. Prioritize self-care: Taking care of yourself physically, mentally, and spiritually is crucial for sustained productivity. Get enough sleep, exercise regularly, maintain healthy eating habits, and find ways to manage stress.

6. Practice effective task management: Utilize tools and techniques that help you stay organized and manage your tasks efficiently. Whether it's using a digital task management app or a simple to-do list, find a system that works for you.

7. Seek accountability and support: Engage with a mentor, colleague, or accountability partner who can help you stay on track and provide encouragement along the way.

Remember, productivity is not just about checking off tasks; it's about achieving meaningful outcomes that align with your vision and goals. By adopting the principle of eating the frog first, you develop discipline, conquer challenges, and unlock your full potential as a children's ministry leader.

As you strive for productivity, it's important to seek divine guidance and inspiration. The Bible offers timeless wisdom in this regard. Proverbs 16:3 states, "Commit to the Lord whatever you do, and He will establish your plans." By aligning your work and productivity with God's guidance, you can trust in his provision and experience the fulfillment that comes from obedience to your calling in children's ministry.

RECRUITING OTHER MEN.

As a man in children's ministry, I have found that it can be easier for me to recruit other men to serve in this area of the church. While many men may not initially consider working with children as their first choice of ministry, I have found that they are often open to the idea when approached by another man.

One reason for this may be that men are more likely to relate to and connect with other men. When men see another man serving in children's ministry, it can break down stereotypes and stigmas that may be associated with this type of work. Men may also feel more comfortable asking questions and seeking advice from other men who have experience in this area.

Another factor may be that men may be more likely to see the value and importance of investing in the next generation. As men, we are called to be leaders and mentors, and serving in children's ministry provides an opportunity to fulfill this role in a meaningful way. When men see the impact they can have on children's lives and the potential for growth and transformation, they may be more willing to step up and serve.

Additionally, men may have unique skills and talents that can be utilized in children's ministry. For example, men may be more comfortable leading outdoor activities, teaching sports, running security, or providing technical support for events. By leveraging the strengths and interests of men, children's ministry programs can be enhanced and made more engaging for both children and volunteers.

However, it's important to note that gender balance is still important in children's ministry teams. While it may be easier for me as a male leader to recruit other men, it's crucial to have a balance of both male and female volunteers. This allows for a diverse range of perspectives and experiences, and provides positive role models for both boys and girls.

Ultimately, serving in children's ministry is a calling that both men and women can answer. It's not about gender, but about a willingness to invest in the next generation and share the love of Christ with them. As a man, I am grateful for the opportunity to recruit and work alongside other men in this important area of ministry, but I also recognize the value and contributions of all volunteers – guys and girls.

A STORY OF GRACE AND MERCY.

The story of David and Mephibosheth is a beautiful illustration of grace and mercy, and it can also provide encouragement to men who serve in kid's ministry. Mephibosheth was the grandson of King Saul, who had been at war with David. Despite the past animosity between their families, David sought to show kindness to Mephibosheth because of the covenant he had made with Jonathan, Mephibosheth's father. David invited Mephibosheth to eat at his table, treating him like a son and providing for his needs.

This story reminds us that God's grace and mercy extend to all, regardless of their background or past mistakes. As children's ministry leaders, we have the opportunity to extend that same grace and kindness to the children we serve. We can create an environment where children feel welcomed and valued, despite their differences or challenges.

Furthermore, David's actions toward Mephibosheth also demonstrate the importance of building relationships in ministry. David could have simply given Mephibosheth some money and sent him on his way, but instead, he invested time and effort into building a relationship with him. Similarly, as children's ministry leaders, we have the opportunity to invest in the lives of the children we serve, building relationships that can have a lasting impact.

Finally, the story of David and Mephibosheth reminds us of the importance of being faithful to the covenant we have with God. David's covenant with Jonathan was a promise to show kindness to Jonathan's family, and David honored that covenant by showing kindness to Mephibosheth. As children's ministry leaders, we have made a covenant with God to serve and love the children He has placed in our care. We must be faithful to that covenant, even when it is challenging or inconvenient.

The story of David and Mephibosheth is a powerful reminder of the importance of extending grace, building relationships, and remaining faithful to our calling in children's ministry. Just as David showed kindness to Mephibosheth despite their past, we can extend the same grace and kindness to the children we serve. By investing in relationships and remaining faithful to our calling, we can make a lasting impact on the lives of the children in our care.

PLUG YOUR EARS.

As men serving in kid's ministry, it can be easy to let the negative voices in your life discourage you. Maybe there are people in your life who don't understand why you are serving in kid's ministry, or who don't value the important work you are doing. Perhaps there are voices in your own head that tell you that you're not good enough or that you should be doing something else.

But as a child of God, you have the power to choose what voices you listen to. The Bible tells us to fix our thoughts on what is true, noble, right, pure, lovely, and admirable (Philippians 4:8). We need to learn to plug our ears to the voices of negativity and focus on the truth of God's Word.

God has called you to serve in kid's ministry, and that is a noble and valuable calling. The work you are doing is making an eternal impact on the lives of the children and families in your church. Don't let the voices of negativity take away from the joy and fulfillment you feel when you see a child grow in his/her faith or when you witness a family coming to know Jesus.

Remember that you are not alone. God is with you, and there are likely other men in your church who are also serving in kid's ministry. Seek out their encouragement and support, and together, you can drown out the voices of negativity with the truth of God's love and purpose for your life.

As you focus on what is true and right, you will find renewed joy and purpose in your ministry to children and families. Keep your eyes fixed on Jesus, the author and perfecter of our faith (Hebrews 12:2), and trust that He will continue to guide and use you for his purposes.

STAYING CONNECTED TO OTHERS.

As men in children's ministry, it's important to stay connected and network with other men who share the same passion and calling. Ministry can be challenging at times, and having a supportive community can make all the difference.

Connecting with other men in children's ministry can provide a space for sharing ideas, resources, and best practices. It can also be an opportunity to learn from one another's successes and failures, and to encourage and pray for each other. When we build relationships with other men, we have access to a network of support that can help us navigate the ups and downs of ministry.

Moreover, connecting with other men in children's ministry can provide a sense of camaraderie and belonging. We were never meant to do ministry alone, and being part of a community can give us a sense of purpose and direction. By working together, we can have a greater impact on the children and families we serve.

Additionally, networking can lead to collaboration on events or projects, which can benefit not only our own ministries, but the community as a whole.

Staying connected and networking with other men in children's ministry is crucial for personal growth, support, and ministry success. Whether it's through attending conferences like The KidzMatter Conference, joining online communities like the I Love Kidmin Facebook Community, or simply reaching out to other men in your church or community; the benefits of networking are numerous. Let's encourage one another and work together to impact the lives of the children and families we serve.

LEADING YOUR TEAM.

In children's ministry, investing in your team and developing leaders is essential. It's not just about getting work done, but it's about empowering others to grow in their faith and calling. As a leader, it's important to recognize the unique strengths and abilities of each team member and provide opportunities for them to utilize and develop those gifts.

One way to invest in your team is through ongoing training and development. This can include attending events, reading books on leadership and ministry, and providing hands-on experience in different areas of children's ministry. Enroll some of your leaders in Kidmin Academy and bring them with you to The KidzMatter Conference. When your team members grow and develop, they will become more confident and equipped to handle challenges and take on leadership roles.

Another important aspect of investing in your team is creating a culture of support and encouragement. This includes regularly affirming team members for their hard work and dedication, providing opportunities for them to share their ideas and feedback, and creating a safe space for open communication and collaboration. When team members feel valued and supported, they will be more engaged and motivated to serve in children's ministry.

As a leader, it's also important to model a servant's heart attitude and prioritize the spiritual growth of your team members. This includes taking time to pray with and for your team members, offering guidance and mentorship, and creating opportunities for them to deepen their relationship with God.

Ultimately, investing in your team is not just about building a strong ministry, but it's about building up the body of Christ. As you invest in your team, you are equipping them to impact the lives of children and families in your church and community, and ultimately, to further the kingdom of God.

KEEPING FIRST THINGS FIRST.

Leading children's ministry is a rewarding and demanding role that requires dedication and passion. However, amidst the busyness of serving others, it's crucial to prioritize and nurture your own spiritual life. Here are some key principles to help you keep your spiritual life a priority while leading in children's ministry:

1. Daily communion with God: Set aside regular time for personal prayer, Bible study, and reflection. Cultivate a deep relationship with God by seeking his presence, listening to his voice, and allowing Him to refresh and renew your spirit.

2. Seek accountability and support: Surround yourself with a community of believers who can provide encouragement, accountability, and support. Engage in small groups, mentoring relationships, or ministry networks where you can share your spiritual journey, seek advice, and pray together.

3. Sabbath rest: Honor the principle of Sabbath by setting aside intentional time for rest, rejuvenation, and worship. Avoid the temptation to constantly be "on" and make time to recharge physically, mentally, and spiritually.

4. Practice spiritual disciplines: Engage in disciplines such as fasting, solitude, worship, and journaling. These practices can help you deepen your intimacy with God, cultivate discernment, and maintain spiritual vitality.

5. Stay connected to the Word: As you prepare lessons and resources for the kids, make sure you personally engage with Scripture. Allow the Word to nourish and guide you, as it will enrich your own spiritual life and provide a solid foundation for teaching and leading others.

6. Embrace vulnerability and transparency: Recognize that you are not exempt from struggles and challenges. Be willing to open up about your own spiritual journey and seek support when needed. Create a culture of authenticity and transparency within your ministry team, allowing for mutual growth and accountability.

7. Maintain healthy boundaries: Learn to prioritize your time and energy, setting healthy boundaries between work, ministry, and personal life. Avoid overextending yourself and be intentional about allocating time for rest, family, and personal growth.

8. Cultivate a grateful heart: Develop an attitude of gratitude and thanksgiving. Celebrate the joys and victories of ministry, even amidst the challenges. Cultivating gratitude will help you maintain perspective, sustain joy, and deepen your spiritual walk.

Remember, your own spiritual health is essential for effectively leading in children's ministry. By prioritizing daily communion with God, seeking accountability, practicing Sabbath rest, engaging in spiritual disciplines, staying connected to the Word, embracing vulnerability, maintaining healthy boundaries, and cultivating gratitude; you will not only nurture your own spiritual life, but also model a vibrant and authentic faith to the kids and families you serve.

A GOD WHO PROVIDES
BEYOND EXPECTATION.

George Mueller, a man of remarkable faith and unwavering dedication, stands as a timeless example of what it means to serve in children's ministry. His life story, documented by many autobiographies, has always captivated my heart and inspired me in my own journey. Every time I leaf through the pages of his remarkable story, I am reminded of the countless ways in which his experiences can encourage and equip men who find themselves leading in children's ministry.

One of the most striking aspects of George Mueller's ministry was his deep trust in God's provision. In an era plagued by financial uncertainties, he embarked on a remarkable journey of faith, establishing orphanages in Bristol, England. Mueller never solicited funds or made his needs known to others, but instead relied solely on God to supply everything required for the care of the children entrusted to him. His unwavering belief that God would faithfully provide for their needs not only resulted in countless miracles, but also demonstrated the profound impact that trust and reliance on God can have in the lives of children's ministry leaders today. In an era where resources may seem scarce, Mueller's story reminds us to place our trust in a God who is able to abundantly provide beyond our expectations.

Moreover, Mueller's unyielding commitment to prayer serves as a powerful example for men in children's ministry leadership. He spent hours each day in fervent communion with God, seeking his wisdom, guidance, and intervention. Mueller believed in the power of prayer to move mountains and transform lives. This emphasis on prayer challenges all of us to cultivate a vibrant prayer life, recognizing that the success of our ministry is intricately linked to our dependence on God through prayer. In the hustle and bustle of ministry, Mueller's example compels us to prioritize communion with our heavenly Father and seek his leading in all that we do.

Another aspect of Mueller's ministry that resonates deeply with me was his genuine love and compassion for children. His commitment to nurturing and caring for the orphans under his care went far beyond meeting their physical needs. Mueller understood the importance of investing in their spiritual growth and guiding them to a personal relationship with Jesus. His heart for the spiritual well-being of children challenges men in children's ministry to go beyond the surface level and invest in the eternal lives of the young ones they serve. Mueller's example reminds us that true impact in children's ministry is not measured solely by numbers, but by the transformational power of God's love in the lives of the little ones we shepherd.

In the life of George Mueller, men serving in children's ministry leadership find a beacon of inspiration and encouragement. His unwavering trust in God's provision, his emphasis on the power of prayer, and his deep love for children are timeless lessons that continue to reverberate in our hearts today. As we navigate the challenges and joys of ministering to children, may we embrace Mueller's legacy as a testament to the transformative power of God and strive to serve with unwavering faith, fervent prayer, and a heart filled with love for the precious souls we have the privilege to influence.

WHAT JESUS THINKS ABOUT CHILDREN'S MINISTRY.

Jesus held children's ministry in high regard, emphasizing its importance and cherishing the little ones. In the Gospels, we find numerous instances where Jesus not only interacted with children, but also highlighted their significance in the kingdom of God.

In Matthew 19:14, Jesus declared, "Let the little children come to me and do not hinder them, for the kingdom of heaven belongs to such as these." This statement underscores the value Jesus placed on children and their place in his ministry. He welcomed them, embraced them, and demonstrated deep care and affection for their well-being. Jesus saw their innocence, purity of heart, and their capacity to believe without reservation.

Furthermore, in Mark 10:13-16, Jesus rebuked his disciples who tried to prevent children from coming to Him, affirming that the kingdom of God belongs to those who receive it with childlike faith. His words and actions reflected his desire to include and bless the little ones, reminding us of the importance of children's ministry in our own lives.

Jesus recognized the immense potential within children, not just as recipients of ministry, but also as examples to learn from. Their simplicity, trust, and openness serve as a model for us as we seek to approach God and grow in our own faith.

Therefore, as children's ministry leaders, we are called to imitate the heart of Jesus. We are to create spaces where children are valued, loved, and nurtured in their spiritual journeys. Just as Jesus welcomed the children, we are to create an environment where they can encounter the love of Christ, grow in their understanding of God's Word, and develop a vibrant relationship with Him.

In following Jesus' example, we affirm the importance of children's ministry as a vital component of the kingdom work. Let's prioritize their spiritual formation, investing our time, talents, and resources to provide them with the guidance and support they need. By embracing Jesus' perspective on children's ministry, we can impact generations, nurturing young disciples who will carry the light of Christ into the world.

INVEST THE TIME AND THE EFFORT.

Maintaining a positive relationship with church leadership and staff is not only crucial, but essential, while serving in children's ministry. As leaders in this capacity, it is critical to be proactive in investing time and effort into building and nurturing these relationships. Doing so not only fosters a sense of unity and collaboration, but also paves the way for a more effective and fruitful ministry. Here are some key reasons why this is paramount and some practical steps to actually make it happen.

First, cultivating a positive relationship with church leadership demonstrates a heart of humility and respect. Recognizing and honoring the authority and guidance of those in leadership positions sets a strong example for those serving with us and under us. Moreover, when leaders see our willingness to work alongside them and support the vision and values of the church, it builds trust and credibility, making us valuable allies in their ministry endeavors. This unity of purpose and mutual respect creates an environment where everyone can work together well, bringing a culture of collaboration and shared mission.

To maintain a positive relationship with church leadership and staff, it is essential to be proactive and intentional in investing time and effort. Seek opportunities to engage with leadership in meaningful ways. Actively engage in staff meetings, participate in church-wide events, and jump in to help whenever possible. By actively seeking ways to contribute beyond the realm of children's ministry, you demonstrate your commitment to the overall vision of the church and your willingness to support the broader mission.

Communication is another vital element in building strong relationships. Take the initiative to regularly communicate with church leadership and staff, keeping them informed about the happenings and successes within the children's ministry. Share testimonies, stories, and updates that showcase the positive impact being made. This not only keeps them in the loop, but also helps them see the value and significance of the work being done with the kids and their families. Additionally, be open and receptive to their feedback, suggestions, and guidance. A willingness to learn and grow demonstrates humility and a genuine desire to improve the ministry.

It is also important to remember that relationships are built on trust and genuine care. Take the time to get to know everyone in leadership on a personal level. Show interest in their lives, families, and ministries. Remember birthdays, anniversaries, and other significant milestones, and extend a genuine word of encouragement or a thoughtful gesture. Building authentic connections fosters a sense of camaraderie and solidarity, strengthening the overall unity of the church body.

I would also encourage you to be mindful of the specific needs and challenges faced by those leading the church. Offer your support and assistance in areas that may not fall directly under your purview. Whether it's helping with event planning, administrative tasks, or volunteering for other ministries; your willingness to serve beyond your immediate responsibilities demonstrates your commitment to the well-being and success of the church as a whole.

By being proactive, investing time, and building authentic relationships; we create an environment of unity, collaboration, and shared mission. Through humility, respect, and effective communication; we demonstrate our commitment to the vision and values of the church, positioning ourselves as valuable allies in the pursuit of the broader mission. Let us approach our relationships with church leadership and staff with intentionality and genuine care, knowing that a strong foundation of trust and mutual support will ultimately lead to a more impactful and fruitful ministry for the children under our care.

IF YOU FAIL TO PREPARE, PREPARE TO FAIL.

The importance of being prepared cannot be overstated. The well-known saying, "If you fail to prepare, you prepare to fail," holds true in various aspects of life, including our roles in children's ministry. Whether we are preparing for a lesson, a meeting, or an event; thorough preparation is paramount. It not only demonstrates our commitment and diligence, but also opens doors for God's blessings to flow.

Preparation allows us to be equipped and ready to fulfill our responsibilities with excellence. When we invest time and effort into studying, planning, and organizing; we are better equipped to deliver impactful lessons, engage effectively in meetings, and execute successful events. By doing our due diligence, we position ourselves to make a lasting difference in the lives of the children and families we serve.

Moreover, God often honors and blesses our preparation. When we diligently prepare and seek his guidance, He can infuse our efforts with wisdom, insight, and creativity beyond our own capabilities. As we commit our plans and preparations to Him, we invite his divine intervention and trust that He will guide our steps and bring about his purposes. God's blessings may manifest in the form of greater impact, meaningful connections, transformed lives, and a sense of his presence and power in our ministry endeavors.

Preparation also brings confidence. I have found that the more prepared I am, the more confident I feel. This confidence allows us to navigate challenges, adapt to unexpected circumstances, and respond effectively to the needs and questions of those we serve. As we step into our roles with prepared hearts and minds, we create an atmosphere of trust and credibility, enabling us to effectively communicate God's truth and love.

However, it's important to remember that preparation should always be accompanied by a posture of dependence on God. While we diligently prepare, we acknowledge that it is ultimately God who works in and through us. Can I get an amen? We seek his guidance, surrendering our plans and preparations to his will. In doing so, we recognize that true success in children's ministry comes not solely from our own efforts, but from the empowering presence and work of the Holy Spirit.

STANDING IN THE GAP.

A powerful example in the Bible of a man who valued children is the story of Elisha and the Shunammite woman found in 2 Kings 4. In this narrative, the Shunammite woman, a notable and respected woman, recognizes Elisha as a holy man of God and decides to provide him with a room in her house whenever he passes through her town. Elisha is deeply grateful for her generosity and wants to show his appreciation.

When Elisha discovers that the Shunammite woman and her husband have been childless and long for a son, he speaks a prophetic word of blessing over her, declaring that she will conceive and bear a son within a year. True to his word, the woman conceives and gives birth to a son. However, tragedy strikes when the child suddenly becomes ill and dies in his mother's arms.

In her anguish, the Shunammite woman seeks out Elisha and lays the lifeless body of her son on the prophet's bed. Elisha, moved with compassion and recognizing the value of this child's life, springs into action. He prays fervently to God, stretches himself out on the boy, and breathes life back into his body. Miraculously, the child comes back to life, and Elisha presents him alive to his mother.

One reason I love this story is that it shows the deep concern and compassion that Elisha had for this child and his mother. Despite the child's tragic death, Elisha believed in the power of God to bring life and restoration. He valued the life of this boy and was willing to intercede on his behalf, demonstrating the importance of children in God's eyes.

Through this story, we see that God's heart is for children and that He values their lives immensely. Elisha's actions remind us of the significance of investing in the next generation, nurturing their faith, and standing in the gap for them. Just like Elisha, men serving in children's ministry have the opportunity to demonstrate God's love, nurture young hearts, and make a lasting impact on their lives.

The example of Elisha and the Shunammite woman's son underscores the importance of recognizing the value of children and actively engaging with them in our ministries. It encourages us to prioritize their spiritual growth, care for their well-being, and be advocates for their flourishing. Just as Elisha esteemed and valued the life of the child, we too must hold children in high regard, recognizing their potential, and investing in their spiritual development.

A SEAT AT THE TABLE.

We all want a seat at the table. What I mean by that is being in a spot where our pastor or leader respects and values our input. While it may take time to establish ourselves as trusted and influential contributors, one of the most powerful ways to achieve this is by consistently showing up. Just show up. By showing up, I am talking about more than being present in the office during office hours. I'm talking about actively engaging in conversations, being a problem solver, and contributing to the overall success of the church ministry. You've got to show up.

If you want a seat at the table, choose to actively participate in discussions and conversations with leadership. Be present not just physically, but also mentally and emotionally. Actively listen to others, seeking to understand their perspectives and insights. Share your thoughts, ideas, and experiences in a respectful and constructive manner. By demonstrating a willingness to engage and contribute, you convey your commitment to the growth and development of the ministry as a whole.

Problem solvers – not bystanders – earn seats at the table. Take the initiative to identify challenges or areas of improvement within the children's ministry or the broader church ministry. Offer practical solutions, propose innovative ideas, and be willing to take on responsibilities to address these issues. This proactive approach not only demonstrates your dedication and passion, but also positions you as a valuable asset and problem-solving partner on the team.

Look for opportunities to lend a helping hand, collaborate with others, and invest in the overall well-being of the church. Support and participate in church-wide initiatives, events, and activities, showing a genuine interest and willingness to serve beyond the boundaries of your specific ministry. By demonstrating a selfless attitude and commitment to the greater mission, you build credibility and influence that extends beyond the realm of children's ministry.

It is important to remember that showing up consistently and making a meaningful impact takes time. It requires patience, perseverance, and humility to earn a seat at the table. Focus on building relationships, earning trust, and demonstrating your commitment over the long term. Consistency in showing up, contributing, and actively engaging in the work of the ministry will gradually establish you as a reliable and respected member of the team.

Earning a seat at the table where our pastor or leader respects and values our input is a journey that requires active participation and contribution. By consistently showing up, actively engaging in conversations, being a problem solver, and contributing to the success of everyone and the entire church ministry; we position ourselves as trusted and influential members of the team. Let's be intentional in our commitment, recognizing that through our consistent presence and positive contributions; we can make a lasting impact on the growth and effectiveness of the children's ministry and the church as a whole.

TEXT ME.

Staying encouraged and inspired is vital as you navigate the joys and challenges of your calling. It fuels passion, creativity, and resilience. To receive a regular dose of encouragement and inspiration, I invite you to text me at (765) 441-4598. I'll add you to my text list. Let's journey together, sharing insights, testimonies, and uplifting stories that will invigorate your ministry. Don't walk this path alone; join a community that uplifts and empowers, reminding you of the incredible impact you're making in the lives of children. Together, we can continue to serve with joy and effectiveness, leaving a lasting legacy in the hearts of the next generation. Text now and let the encouragement begin!

A CHICK-FIL-A EXPERIENCE.

I love Chick-fil-A. Do you? I love their food (and sweet tea) and their customer service, as well as their attention to the details. Just as Chick-fil-A is known for their warm hospitality, we can create a welcoming and friendly environment in our ministry. Embracing a servant-hearted approach, we can go above and beyond to meet the needs of children and families, ensuring they feel valued and cared for. Moreover, like Chick-fil-A's attention to detail in their operations; we should strive for excellence in all aspects of our children's ministry, from curriculum development to event planning. By focusing on quality and consistency, we can create impactful experiences that leave a lasting impression. Additionally, Chick-fil-A's emphasis on strong core values can inspire us to instill biblical principles and values in our ministry, guiding children towards a vibrant faith. Let's learn from Chick-fil-A's dedication to customer service, attention to detail, and core values; then apply these principles to create an amazing children's ministry experience.

PUT YOURSELF OUT THERE.

Putting yourself out there and taking risks is a vital aspect of personal growth and success, especially when serving in children's ministry. Stepping beyond our comfort zones and embracing calculated risks opens doors to new opportunities and allows us to make a meaningful impact on the lives of the children and families we serve.

By taking risks, we challenge ourselves to grow, learn, and innovate. Trying new teaching methods, exploring creative ways to engage children, or venturing into uncharted territories within the ministry can yield transformative results. It may involve stepping up to lead a new program, organizing a community outreach event, or initiating partnerships with other churches. These risks can lead to breakthroughs in how we connect with kids, share the Gospel, and foster a vibrant and inclusive ministry environment.

Taking risks also demonstrates our commitment and passion. When we are willing to go beyond what is expected, to push boundaries, and to navigate unfamiliar territory; we communicate our genuine dedication to the children and the ministry. Our boldness and willingness to take risks inspire others, encouraging them to step out of their own comfort zones and join us in making a difference.

Moreover, embracing risks allows us to learn from both successes and failures. Each risk taken provides valuable lessons and insights, contributing to our personal and professional growth. Through these experiences, we develop resilience, adaptability, and an entrepreneurial spirit that strengthens our ability to lead and serve effectively.

In children's ministry, the impact of taking risks goes beyond our own personal growth and development. It creates a culture of innovation, openness, and continuous improvement. Your willingness to take risks and try new things is contagious! It inspires others to bring their ideas, talents, and unique contributions to the table, resulting in a more vibrant and impactful ministry.

Be bold, innovative, and willing to take risks as you strive to serve and impact the lives of the kids you have the privilege of ministering to.

CREATE A UNIFIED FRONT.

Ensuring that your vision is aligned with your pastor's vision is of huge importance. By staying in sync with your pastor's vision, supporting it wholeheartedly, and intentionally aligning your visions; you create a unified front that can maximize impact and grow the church.

Make sure you are regularly communicating with your pastor to gain a deep understanding of his (or her) vision for the church.

Actively listen to sermons, actively listen in staff meetings, and engage in conversations to discern his heart and passion. Seek clarity on how the children's ministry can contribute to the overarching mission and values of the church. By developing a strong understanding of your pastor's vision, you can align your ministry goals and activities accordingly.

Supporting your pastor's vision is paramount. It requires a genuine commitment to the success of the overall church ministry rather than focusing solely on the children's ministry. Recognize that your role is part of a bigger picture, and be willing to make adjustments, sacrifices, and investments that align with the bigger vision. This may involve realigning priorities, reallocating resources, and seeking ways to integrate the children's ministry into the church's overall strategy.

To align visions, it is crucial to establish open lines of communication and collaboration with leadership. Regularly engage in intentional conversations to share updates, seek feedback, and gain alignment on key initiatives. Invite your pastor's input and insight into the planning and decision-making processes of big children's ministry decisions. By involving him and seeking his guidance, you ensure that your actions and strategies are aligned with his vision.

I want to mention the power of prayer in aligning visions. Seek God's guidance and wisdom as you align the children's ministry with your pastor's vision. Pray for discernment, unity, and clarity of purpose. Surrender your plans and desires to God, trusting that He will lead and guide your steps. Proverbs 16:3 reminds us, "Commit to the Lord whatever you do, and He will establish your plans." By committing your ministry endeavors to God and aligning them with your pastor's vision, you invite his blessings and enable his purposes to prevail.

Remember, as you align your children's ministry with your pastor's vision, you create a unified front that can maximize the impact of the church and bring glory to God.

PUT YOURSELF IN THEIR SHOES.

Practicing empathy, especially towards your volunteers, is a crucial aspect of effective leadership in children's ministry. When you put yourself in their shoes, seeking to understand their perspectives, emotions, and needs; it can make a significant difference in how you interact with them, pray for them, make requests of them, and ultimately lead them.

By empathizing with your volunteers, you develop a deeper appreciation for their commitment, sacrifices, and contributions. Recognize that they are giving their time, energy, and talents out of a genuine desire to serve and make a difference. Understand the challenges they may face, such as juggling multiple responsibilities, overcoming personal obstacles, or dealing with the demands of their own lives. This understanding allows you to approach them with compassion, sensitivity, and respect.

Empathy also influences how you pray for your team. As you step into their shoes and gain insight into their experiences; you can pray more specifically and earnestly for their needs, joys, and struggles. Pray for their spiritual growth, emotional well-being, and personal lives. Lift up their concerns, celebrate their victories, and intercede for God's provision and guidance in their service. By praying empathetically, you demonstrate your care and concern for their overall well-being.

Empathy also affects how you make requests of your volunteers. Understanding their perspectives helps you tailor your communication and requests to their specific needs and capacities. Consider the challenges they may face, and be mindful of their limitations and boundaries. Be clear and concise in your expectations, providing the necessary support, resources, and training to enable their success. By making requests with empathy, you create an environment of understanding and collaboration, fostering a sense of unity and shared purpose.

Leading with empathy means taking the time to listen, understand, and respond to the needs of your volunteers. Create opportunities for open dialogue, allowing them to express their thoughts, concerns, and ideas. Be responsive to their feedback and suggestions, acknowledging and incorporating their input where appropriate. By leading with empathy, you build trust, respect, and a strong sense of community among your volunteers.

YOU AREN'T ALONE.

As children's pastors, it is essential to remember that you are never alone in your ministry journey. The Holy Spirit, the very presence of God, is always with you, guiding, empowering, and equipping you for the task at hand. Understanding the role of the Holy Spirit in your life as a ministry leader can bring comfort, confidence, and a renewed sense of purpose.

The Holy Spirit serves as your constant companion and counselor. He provides wisdom, discernment, and direction as you make decisions, plan lessons, and navigate the complexities of ministry. Jesus promised his disciples the gift of the Holy Spirit, who would be their advocate and guide. In John 14:26, Jesus said, "But the Advocate, the Holy Spirit, whom the Father will send in my name, will teach you all things and will remind you of everything I have said to you." Trust in the Holy Spirit's guidance, knowing that He will lead you in the way you should go.

The Holy Spirit also empowers you with supernatural strength and abilities. Ministry can be demanding, and at times, you may feel inadequate or overwhelmed. However, the Holy Spirit equips you with the spiritual gifts necessary for your role as a children's pastor. These gifts, such as teaching, leadership, wisdom, and encouragement enable you to serve with excellence and impact the lives of the kids and families you minister to. Embrace the Holy Spirit's empowerment, relying on his strength to fulfill your calling.

Additionally, the Holy Spirit brings comfort, peace, and encouragement in times of difficulty or discouragement. This paragraph right here may be the one thing you need to hear from this whole book. Ministry is challenging. You will encounter setbacks, opposition, or moments of doubt. However, the Holy Spirit is your source of comfort and encouragement, reminding you of God's faithfulness and empowering you to persevere. Romans 8:26 assures us, "In the same way, the Spirit helps us in our weakness. We do not know what we ought to pray for, but the Spirit Himself intercedes for us through wordless groans." Lean on the Holy Spirit's intercession and find solace in his presence.

Remember that as a children's pastor, you are never alone. The Holy Spirit is always with you - guiding, empowering, comforting, and transforming you for the ministry. Rely on the Holy Spirit's guidance, tap into his empowerment, and find solace in his presence. Allow Him to work in and through you, knowing that He is faithfully leading and equipping you to impact the lives of the children you serve. Take comfort in the words of Joshua 1:9, "Have I not commanded you? Be strong and courageous. Do not be afraid; do not be discouraged, for the LORD your God will be with you wherever you go."

TELEPHONE OR MEGAPHONE?

When it comes to using social media in your children's ministry, it's important to approach it as a telephone rather than a megaphone. In other words, use it as a tool to build conversations and foster community, rather than solely making announcements and trying to be heard.

Social media provides a unique opportunity to connect with parents, volunteers, and the broader church community on a regular basis. Instead of simply broadcasting information, engage in meaningful conversations that invite interaction and participation. Pose questions, share thought-provoking content, and respond to comments and messages. By using social media as a telephone, you create an environment where people feel valued, heard, and connected.

Additionally, social media can serve as a platform for building community. Encourage discussions and collaboration among parents and volunteers. Facilitate online groups where they can share insights, resources, and prayer requests. Celebrate successes, highlight individual stories, and acknowledge the contributions of your community members. By focusing on building relationships and fostering a sense of belonging, you can create a vibrant online community that extends beyond the physical boundaries of your ministry.

Remember, social media is not just a one-way communication channel. It is a powerful tool that, when used intentionally, can help cultivate a sense of community, nurture relationships, and provide a platform for meaningful conversations. Embrace the opportunity to connect, engage, and listen through social media; and watch as it enhances the impact and effectiveness of your children's ministry.

STAYING SHARP.

The choice to grow and improve daily helps you stay relevant, effective, and impactful in your roles. Just as a blade needs sharpening to maintain its cutting edge, you too must commit to ongoing development and growth.

One biblical example of someone who prioritized personal growth is the apostle Paul. Throughout his ministry, Paul demonstrated a relentless pursuit of growth and improvement. In his letter to the Philippians, he wrote, "Not that I have already obtained all this, or have already arrived at my goal, but I press on to take hold of that for which Christ Jesus took hold of me" (Philippians 3:12). Paul recognized that his journey of faith and ministry was a continual process of growth and transformation. He never settled for complacency, but remained focused on pressing forward and taking hold of God's calling on his life.

To stay sharp, you need to adopt a growth mindset and embrace various strategies for personal development. These may include:

1. Continuous Learning: Engage in regular study and exploration of relevant topics, attending conferences like The KidzMatter Conference, taking a Kidmin Academy course, reading books, and seeking out resources that broaden your knowledge and understanding.

2. Seeking Feedback: Be open to feedback from others, seeking input from mentors, peers, and those you serve. Embrace constructive criticism as an opportunity for growth and improvement.

3. Embracing Challenges: Step out of your comfort zone, taking on new challenges that stretch your abilities and expand your skill set. Embrace opportunities that push you to grow and develop as a leader.

4. Building a Network: Surround yourself with a supportive network of fellow ministry leaders, mentors, and colleagues. Engage in discussions on KidzMatter's I Love Kidmin Facebook Community, share insights, and learn from one another's experiences.

5. Reflective Practice: Set aside regular time for self-reflection and evaluation. Consider what worked well or areas for needed improvement, and then make intentional adjustments to enhance your effectiveness.

6. Embracing Innovation: Stay on top of emerging trends, technological advancements, and innovative approaches in children's ministry. Embrace new tools and strategies that can enhance your ministry impact.

By choosing growth and making intentional efforts to improve, you ensure that you remain effective and adaptable in your roles. As you follow the example of Paul and commit to staying sharp, you position yourself to better serve the children and families you minister to, advancing the kingdom of God through your continuous growth and development.

THE IMPACT YOU'RE MAKING.

George MacDonald's timeless quote resonates deeply with men serving in children's ministry: "I doubt whether anyone can be called a true Christian who does not feel his heart beat with the love of little children, and who cannot forgive their faults as freely as their Maker forgives his own." Embracing this sentiment, you understand that children are not just the future of the Church but an integral part of its present. Your dedication to serving in children's ministry is a beautiful reflection of your commitment and love for the next generation. As you see kids running the halls of your church, be reminded that their presence signifies the impact you're making. Embrace this opportunity to shape hearts, ignite faith, and show God's love. Through your commitment, you leave a lasting imprint on their hearts and lives.

SERVING SOMEONE ELSE'S VISION.

Pursuing the vision that God has given you while staying aligned with your pastor's vision can present a unique challenge, but it is an essential aspect of effective ministry. It requires navigating the delicate balance between pursuing your ideas and vision while remaining submitted to the leadership and direction set by the church. Here are some principles to consider in navigating this challenge:

First, cultivate a heart of humility and submission. Recognize that you are part of a larger body and that serving the vision of the house is a vital contribution to the overall mission of the church. Philippians 2:3-4 reminds us, "Do nothing out of selfish ambition or vain conceit. Rather, in humility value others above yourselves, not looking to your own interests but each of you to the interests of the others." Prioritize the vision of the church and align your own ideas and desires accordingly.

Second, communicate and collaborate with your leaders. Seek to understand the vision and direction set by the church leadership. Engage in open dialogue, share your ideas, and respectfully express your perspectives. Proverbs 15:22 advises, "Plans fail for lack of counsel, but with many advisers, they succeed." By involving your leaders in the process, you can find ways to integrate your ideas into the overarching vision or gain insights on how to refine them to better align with the church's direction.

Third, be flexible and adaptable. Recognize that your pastor's vision may evolve or change over time, and you need to be willing to adjust accordingly. Remain open to feedback, course corrections, and redirection from your leaders. Trust in the Lord's guidance and surrender your personal aspirations for the greater good of the church's vision.

Finally, commit to excellence in serving your pastor's vision. Regardless of whether it aligns perfectly with your personal ideas and vision, give your best effort, skills, and resources to support and advance the overarching mission. My life verse is Colossians 3:23 and it encourages us, "Whatever you do, work at it with all your heart, as working for the Lord." Remember that ultimately, you are serving God, and your faithfulness and commitment to the vision of the church can bring about God's blessings and fruitfulness.

THE BUTTERFLY EFFECT.

The butterfly effect is a concept in chaos theory that suggests that small, seemingly insignificant actions can have far-reaching and profound consequences. It was discovered by meteorologist Edward Lorenz, who noticed that even tiny changes in initial conditions could lead to drastically different outcomes in weather patterns.

The butterfly effect serves as a powerful reminder of the impact you have. Every interaction, lesson, and act of kindness, no matter how small, can create a ripple effect that influences the lives of the children you serve. Even the smallest gesture or word of encouragement can shape their faith journey.

Seize every opportunity to sow seeds of love, faith, and truth, trusting that God can use these small acts to bring about significant transformations in the lives of kids and their families. Your ministry, even in seemingly insignificant moments, can contribute to the greater work that God is doing in his Kingdom.

PARENTS NEED YOU.

Children's pastors play a vital role in supporting parents within the church. Today's families face numerous challenges as they raise kids in a fast-changing world. You can make a difference by offering guidance, encouragement, and resources to those parents. Many parents struggle with the busyness of life, balancing work, unending household tasks, and caring for their kids. You can provide a nurturing environment where parents can find community, spiritual nourishment, and connection with God. You can also help parents navigate the influence of secular culture by providing biblical teachings and practical parenting advice. Parents may also question their abilities, and you can offer reassurance, encouragement, and biblical wisdom, reminding them to seek God's guidance. When serving parents in these ways, you are making a lasting impact on families, shaping the future generation and fostering a solid foundation of faith. Parents need you!

SPINNING MULTIPLE PLATES.

As a children's ministry leader, you have numerous responsibilities and tasks to manage. From preparing lessons and recruiting volunteers to creating resources for parents and planning events; it can feel like you're spinning multiple plates simultaneously. However, with effective strategies in place, you can stay organized and manage these responsibilities efficiently. Here are some key principles to consider:

First and foremost, set clear priorities. Understand the essential aspects of your ministry that require immediate attention and focus. Identify the tasks that have the most significant impact on your ministry. By prioritizing your activities, you can allocate your time and energy effectively, ensuring that the most critical areas receive the attention they deserve.

Delegation is crucial for managing multiple responsibilities. Recognize that you don't have to do everything yourself. Empower and involve others in your ministry team by delegating tasks and responsibilities. Identify individuals with specific skills or interests who can take on various aspects of the ministry, whether it's lesson preparation, event planning, or administrative tasks. Delegating not only lightens your workload, but also allows others to contribute their gifts and talents, creating a sense of ownership and teamwork.

Staying organized is key to effectively managing multiple plates. Utilize tools and systems that work best for you such as digital calendars, task management apps, or project management software. Develop a system for tracking deadlines, scheduling meetings, and managing resources. Regularly review and update your organizational system to ensure it remains relevant and effective for you.

Time management is essential in juggling multiple responsibilities. Set aside dedicated time for specific tasks and avoid multitasking excessively, as it can often lead to decreased productivity. Establish a routine that includes focused blocks of time for lesson preparation, volunteer recruitment, and other important activities. By managing your time wisely, you can optimize your productivity and reduce the likelihood of feeling overwhelmed.

Remember to take care of yourself. Self-care is vital for sustaining your energy and passion as a ministry leader. Prioritize rest, healthy boundaries, and personal renewal. Seek support from others and lean on your ministry team for encouragement and assistance when needed. By taking care of yourself, you will be better equipped to manage the multiple plates of your ministry effectively.

Proverbs 16:3 reminds us, "Commit to the LORD whatever you do, and He will establish your plans." By committing your ministry efforts to God and seeking his guidance, you can find wisdom, strength, and direction in managing your responsibilities.

OVERCOMING HURDLES IN MINISTRY.

In the world of children's ministry, overcoming hurdles can be a daunting task. As children's ministry leaders, we often encounter challenges that require us to think strategically and find innovative solutions. One powerful approach to tackling these hurdles is by learning to ask the right questions. That's why John Maxwell wrote the book Good Leaders Ask Great Questions. By embracing the art of questioning, we can unlock hidden insights, gain clarity, and discover fresh perspectives that enable us to overcome obstacles in ministry.

If you are going to ask good questions, you have to start by challenging assumptions. It's easy to operate based on assumptions and preconceived notions. However, by questioning these assumptions, we open ourselves up to new possibilities and broaden our understanding of the hurdles we face. Jesus Himself was a master at challenging assumptions, using thought-provoking questions that compelled people to reevaluate their beliefs and perspectives.

Another vital aspect is asking questions that bring understanding. Instead of jumping to conclusions or superficially addressing the surface-level issues, we should dig deeper and seek to comprehend the root causes and underlying factors contributing to the hurdles. By asking open-ended questions and encouraging dialogue, we create a space for people to share their thoughts, experiences, and concerns.

Asking questions that inspire creativity and innovation is also important. By challenging conventional thinking and encouraging brainstorming, we open things up for new ideas. Proverbs 25:2 reminds us that seeking out matters is the glory of kings, emphasizing the importance of exploring uncharted territories and discovering innovative approaches. Through creative questioning, we can unlock previously unconsidered possibilities and find unique solutions to the hurdles we face.

One of the biggest lessons I have learned when it comes to asking good questions is not to ask them alone. The more I involve my ministry team, volunteers, and even the kids themselves; the better off I am. By asking questions that invite their input, suggestions, and ideas; I create a collaborative environment.

The art of asking the right questions is a powerful tool for overcoming hurdles in ministry. Ask bad questions and you'll get bad answers. Ask good questions and get good answers. Ask great questions and you'll get great answers! Embracing the spirit of questioning allows us to uncover hidden insights, discover innovative solutions, and fulfill God's calling in our children's ministry.

WHEN TO STAY AND WHEN TO GO.

I can't tell you how many times I get asked the question, "How do I know when it's time to stay or time to go?" Deciding when to stay or leave a ministry can be a challenging and gut-wrenching decision for children's pastors. It's not an easy question to answer, but I'm going to try to help you navigate this. It's important to seek guidance from trusted friends, prayerfully consider the situation, and ultimately trust your gut, guided by God's wisdom. Here are some key considerations for navigating this decision:

First, seek wise counsel from people you know and trust. Share your thoughts and concerns with mentors, fellow ministry leaders, or spiritual advisors who can provide valuable insights and perspectives. Proverbs 11:14 reminds us, "For lack of guidance a nation falls, but victory is won through many advisers." Engaging in open and honest conversations can help shed light on your situation and provide valuable input.

Secondly, prioritize prayer in discerning your path. Seek God's guidance and wisdom through prayer, asking for clarity and direction. Philippians 4:6-7 encourages us, "Do not be anxious about anything, but in every situation, by prayer and petition, with thanksgiving, present your requests to God. And the peace of God, which transcends all understanding, will guard your hearts and your minds in Christ Jesus." As you pray, ask for discernment and a sense of peace regarding your decision.

Additionally, reflect on your personal circumstances and reasons for considering a change. Evaluate your current ministry's alignment with your gifts, passions, and calling. Consider the impact you're making, the growth opportunities available, and the overall health of the ministry. Trust your gut instincts and pay attention to any signs of dissatisfaction or restlessness that may indicate a need for change.

It's also essential to assess the support and resources available to you. Evaluate the leadership dynamics, the team's compatibility, and the level of support you receive from the church community. Consider if there are opportunities for growth and if your vision aligns with the church's vision. Proverbs 15:22 advises, "Plans fail for lack of counsel, but with many advisers, they succeed." Evaluate if the current ministry environment provides the necessary support and resources for your effectiveness and growth.

While external factors play a role, ultimately, it's vital to listen to God's voice within you. Trust that the Holy Spirit will guide and direct your steps. Proverbs 3:5-6 reminds us, "Trust in the LORD with all your heart and lean not on your own understanding; in all your ways submit to Him, and He will make your paths straight." Allow God's wisdom to illuminate your decision-making process and give you the assurance you need.

Deciding when to stay or leave a ministry requires seeking wise counsel, praying for guidance, reflecting on personal circumstances, and listening to the prompting of the Holy Spirit. Engage in open conversations, seek God's wisdom through prayer, and trust your intuition, guided by biblical principles. Remember that God's plans for you are good, and as you seek his guidance, He will make your paths straight.

THE MOST IMPORTANT WORK.

Children's ministry holds a position of utmost importance and urgency within the church. It plays a vital role in shaping the foundation of children's faith and has a profound impact on their lifelong spiritual journey. Jesus Himself emphasized the significance of children, reminding us in Matthew 19:14, "Let the little children come to me, and do not hinder them, for the kingdom of heaven belongs to such as these."

Children's ministry is a strategic opportunity to sow seeds of truth, love, and the Gospel into the lives of young hearts. During childhood, children are receptive and impressionable, eager to learn and explore. By engaging them in age-appropriate teachings, worship, and discipleship; we have the privilege of instilling in them a strong foundation of biblical knowledge and a personal relationship with Jesus Christ.

Furthermore, children's ministry holds the key to the future of the Church. As we invest in the spiritual development of children, we are not only impacting their lives, but also shaping the destiny of the Church as a whole. Proverbs 22:6 encourages us with these words, "Start children off on the way they should go, and even when they are old they will not turn from it." By nurturing their faith and discipleship at an early age, we equip them to become faithful and resilient followers of Christ, who will in turn impact future generations with the Gospel.

Children's ministry also has the potential to reach families and communities with the transformative power of Christ. Children often bring their parents to church, providing a unique opportunity to engage families in the life of the church and share the love of Jesus with them. Through intentional outreach, parent partnerships, and community engagement; children's ministry becomes a gateway for spreading the Good News and bringing the kingdom of God to bear on the lives of families.

Children's ministry also allows us to witness the work of the Holy Spirit in the lives of kids. We have the privilege of seeing their hearts open to God's love, their faith blossom, and their lives transformed by his grace. Jesus affirms the importance of childlike faith in Matthew 18:3, saying, "Truly I tell you, unless you change and become like little children, you will never enter the kingdom of heaven." Children's ministry provides a nurturing environment where children can experience the power of God's Spirit, fostering a genuine and vibrant relationship with Him.

I believe that children's ministry is the most vital and urgent ministry in the church. It shapes the foundation of a child's faith, impacts future generations, reaches families and communities, and provides a unique opportunity to witness the work of the Holy Spirit. As we invest in children's spiritual development, we fulfill the call to nurture young hearts, equipping them to be faithful disciples who carry the torch of God's kingdom into the future.

YOU ARE MORE CREATIVE THAN YOU THINK.

You may not naturally consider yourself creative, but I have good news! It's important to remember that creativity is not limited to artistic abilities or extravagant ideas. Creativity in ministry is about finding innovative ways to engage with children, communicate biblical truths, and make a lasting impact on their lives. Here are some practical ways to keep your creative juices flowing and be effective in children's ministry:

1. Embrace a growth mindset: Cultivate a mindset that believes creativity can be developed and expanded. Recognize that creativity is not fixed, but can be nurtured through practice and learning. Embrace a willingness to try new things, take risks, and learn from both successes and failures.

2. Seek inspiration from others: Surround yourself with creative influences. Read books, blogs, and articles on children's ministry, attend conferences like The KidzMatter Conference, and connect with other ministry leaders. Draw inspiration from their ideas, experiences, and approaches. Collaborate and learn from one another.

3. Connect with the kids: Spend time with the kids and families in your ministry. Engage in conversations, listen to their thoughts, and observe their interests. Understanding their unique perspectives and needs will spark creative ideas on how to effectively teach and minister to them.

4. Think outside the box: Challenge yourself to think beyond the conventional methods of ministry. Explore different teaching techniques, interactive activities, games, and visual aids that resonate with kids. Consider how you can incorporate technology, arts and crafts, storytelling, drama, or music to enhance your lessons and captivate their attention.

5. Involve your team: Collaboration can generate innovative ideas. Foster an environment where your ministry team can brainstorm and share their creativity. Encourage everyone to contribute their unique strengths, perspectives, and ideas. Together, you can generate fresh and engaging approaches in ministering to children.

6. Stay updated: Keep yourself informed about the latest trends, resources, and tools in children's ministry. Attend workshops, webinars, and training sessions to learn new techniques and gather ideas. Continuously seek opportunities for personal and professional growth to stay relevant and creative in your ministry approach.

7. Embrace simplicity: Remember that creativity doesn't always require elaborate set-ups or grandiose ideas. Sometimes, the most impactful moments come from simplicity. Focus on clear and concise communication of biblical truths, incorporating meaningful activities, and creating an environment where children feel safe, loved, and valued.

8. Pray for creativity: Seek God's guidance and inspiration through prayer. Ask the Holy Spirit to stir your creativity

and provide fresh ideas that align with his purpose. Recognize that God is the ultimate Creator and the source of all inspiration. Trust in his ability to work through you and bring forth creative solutions for effective ministry.

9. Reflect and evaluate: Regularly reflect on your ministry efforts and evaluate their effectiveness. Ask for feedback from the children, parents, and your ministry team. Assess what works well and what can be improved upon. Embrace a mindset of continuous learning and adaptation.

Remember, creativity in children's ministry is not about being the most artistic or having the flashiest ideas. You – as a man in children's ministry – can be creative! By embracing a growth mindset, seeking inspiration, connecting with kids, thinking outside the box, involving your team, staying updated, embracing simplicity, praying for creativity, and reflecting on your efforts; you can keep your creative juices flowing and make a lasting impact in children's lives.

HAVE A GROWTH MINDSET.

Having a growth mindset is the idea that our abilities, talents, and intelligence can be developed through dedication, hard work, and a willingness to learn. It is the understanding that our potential is not fixed, but can expand with effort and perseverance. For children's pastors and ministry leaders, cultivating a growth mindset is imperative for personal growth, effective leadership, and impacting the lives of children.

With a growth mindset, you are more inclined to embrace challenges, view obstacles as opportunities for growth, and persist in the face of setbacks. You are not deterred by failures, but rather you see them as stepping stones to improvement. This mindset encourages a lifelong pursuit of knowledge, innovation, and personal development which directly impacts the quality of your ministry.

A growth mindset also enhances your leadership effectiveness. By continuously seeking to expand your skills, knowledge, and understanding; you can adapt to changing circumstances, think creatively, and lead with agility. You are open to feedback, value collaboration, and inspire those around you to embrace growth and reach their potential.

In 2 Peter 3:18, we are encouraged to "grow in the grace and knowledge of our Lord and Savior Jesus Christ." This verse reminds us of the importance of continual growth in our faith and ministry. A growth mindset aligns with this biblical principle, as it encourages us to embrace a posture of growth in all aspects of our lives.

Furthermore, having a growth mindset is crucial for children's pastors and ministry leaders because you play a pivotal role in shaping the spiritual development of children. By modeling a growth mindset, you inspire children to embrace challenges, develop resilience, and believe in their potential to grow in their relationship with God.

Ultimately, having a growth mindset as a children's pastor or ministry leader is not only personally fulfilling, but also instrumental in cultivating a culture of growth, learning, and spiritual development within the ministry. It empowers you to adapt to the ever-changing needs of kids, innovate in your approaches, and positively impact the lives of those you serve.

YOU NEED A COACH.

Having a coach as a children's ministry leader can be an invaluable asset to your personal growth, leadership effectiveness, and ministry impact. A coach provides an objective perspective, accountability, guidance, and support that can propel your ministry forward.

To find a coach, start by seeking recommendations from trusted colleagues, mentors, or other ministry leaders who have worked with coaches before. Their insights and recommendations can help you find coaches who align with your needs and goals. Additionally, attending conferences and workshops focused on children's ministry can provide opportunities to connect with experienced leaders and potential coaches who specialize in ministry leadership.

Networking within ministry circles is another effective way to find a coach. Engaging in networking events, both in-person and online, allows you to connect with other children's ministry leaders who may have recommendations or be able to point you in the right direction.

Exploring coaching organizations that focus on ministry leadership or offer coaching services specifically tailored to children's ministry can also be fruitful. These organizations often have directories or platforms to help you find qualified coaches.

Having a coach can provide valuable insights, guidance, and support as you navigate the challenges and opportunities of children's ministry leadership. Their expertise and outside perspective can help you grow as a leader, enhance your ministry impact, and ultimately transform the lives of the kids you serve.

WHO CAN YOU MENTOR?

Being a mentor to younger people aspiring to serve in children's ministry is rewarding and impactful. It allows you to share your wisdom, experience, and passion while equipping the next generation of leaders. To be an effective mentor, focus on building a relationship with your mentees. Take the time to get to know them personally; understand their strengths, interests, and aspirations. This genuine connection forms the foundation for meaningful mentorship.

Share your experiences in children's ministry to provide valuable insights. Draw from your own challenges, victories, and lessons learned. By sharing your stories, you can inspire and guide them along their own journey. Additionally, offer practical guidance and resources to help them develop their skills and knowledge in children's ministry. Recommend relevant books, podcasts, conferences (I know a good one!), and training opportunities that can enhance their understanding and effectiveness.

Create opportunities for mentees to actively engage in ministry. Involve them in planning events, leading lessons, or organizing outreach programs. Practical experience is invaluable in shaping their skills and building confidence. Act as a sounding board for mentees, offering a safe and open space for them to share their ideas, concerns, and questions. Listen attentively, provide feedback, and offer constructive criticism when needed. Help them grow through challenges and learn from their mistakes.

Celebrate the achievements and milestones of your mentees. Acknowledge their growth and dedication, showing genuine appreciation for their efforts. This fosters a sense of accomplishment and encourages them to continue serving in children's ministry with passion and excellence. By being a mentor, you have the privilege to make a lasting impact on the next generation of children's ministry leaders, helping them grow in their faith and equipping them to impact the lives of children in powerful ways.

BATTLING LONELINESS IN MINISTRY.

Battling loneliness in ministry is a common struggle that we all face at times. The weight of responsibility, the challenges of the role, and the sense of isolation can make you feel alone. However, it is important to remember that you aren't alone! The story of Elijah offers encouragement and a reminder that even in our loneliest moments, we are never truly alone.

In 1 Kings 19, we find Elijah feeling discouraged and isolated. He had just witnessed a great victory, but now he faced threats and opposition. Fearing for his life, he fled to the wilderness and asked God to take his life. In his darkest moment, God revealed Himself to Elijah in a gentle whisper, reminding him that he was not alone. God assured Elijah that He had preserved a remnant of faithful people and that Elijah was not the only one remaining.

This story serves as a powerful reminder that even when we feel isolated and alone in ministry, God is with us. He sees our struggles, understands our feelings, and provides the strength and encouragement we need to persevere. It is essential to lean on God through prayer, seeking his presence, and allowing his comforting whispers to remind us of his faithfulness.

Additionally, battling loneliness in ministry can be helped by seeking support from others. Connect with fellow ministry leaders, pastors, or trusted friends who can provide a listening ear, wise counsel, and empathy. Consider joining a ministry network or seeking out a mentor who can offer guidance and support.

Remember, God is always present, even in our loneliest moments. He is our ultimate source of comfort and strength. By staying connected to Him and seeking community with others, we can navigate the challenges of ministry and find solace in the knowledge that we are never truly alone.

LEADERS ARE COMMUNICATORS.

The power of communication cannot be overstated, especially as a children's pastor. Effective communication enables you to connect, inspire, and influence those you serve. Whether it's conveying a message to a small group of children, sharing with a congregation, or presenting ideas to other leaders on your team; honing our communication skills is essential. Here are some key principles to become a better communicator:

1. Clarity and simplicity: Strive for clarity in your message by organizing your thoughts and delivering them in a concise manner. Use simple and understandable language, avoiding unnecessary jargon or complex terms. Consider the needs and understanding of your audience.

2. Active listening: Communication is a two-way process. Practice active listening to truly understand others' perspectives, needs, and concerns. Engage in genuine dialogue, asking questions, and providing space for others to share their thoughts. This fosters deeper connections and meaningful communication.

3. Nonverbal communication: Remember that communication extends beyond words. Pay attention to your body language, facial expressions, and tone of voice. Maintain eye contact, use gestures purposefully, and convey warmth and empathy through your nonverbal cues.

4. Adaptability: Recognize that different situations and audiences require different communication approaches. Adapt your style, tone, and delivery to effectively engage and connect with diverse individuals and groups. Flexibility enhances your ability to connect and resonate with others.

5. Practice and feedback: Continuously refine your communication skills through practice. Seek opportunities

to present, teach, or lead in various settings. Embrace constructive feedback from others, incorporating their insights to improve your communication skills.

6. Use storytelling: Stories have the power to captivate, inspire, and convey messages in a memorable way. Jesus was a master at storytelling. Incorporate storytelling techniques to engage your audience emotionally and make your message relatable. Craft narratives that illustrate key points or share personal experiences that resonate with others.

7. Empathy and sensitivity: Cultivate empathy and sensitivity in your communication. Consider the perspectives and feelings of others. Tailor your message to address the needs and concerns of your audience, demonstrating genuine care and understanding.

8. Seek growth opportunities: Continuously seek resources, books, or podcasts that can enhance your communication skills.

Remember, effective communication is a lifelong journey of growth and improvement. Embrace every opportunity to refine your skills, whether it's writing an email, speaking to a small group, or addressing a larger audience. By sharpening your communication abilities, you will become a more influential and impactful leader, connecting with others in powerful ways and effectively fulfilling your ministry's mission.

STOP DOING IT ALL - START DELEGATING

The power and importance of delegating tasks to others cannot be underestimated, especially for leaders in children's ministry. Delegation not only lightens the load, but also empowers and develops the capabilities of those around you. It allows you to focus on essential responsibilities while creating a sense of ownership and growth in your team.

Delegating tasks enables you to leverage the unique talents and skills of others, promoting collaboration and synergy within the ministry. It empowers individuals to contribute their gifts, creativity, and expertise fostering a sense of shared ownership and commitment to the ministry's vision.

One biblical principle that highlights the significance of delegation is found in Exodus 18:17-23. In this passage, Moses faces the challenge of managing the burdensome task of judging and resolving disputes for the Israelites. His father-in-law, Jethro, wisely advises him to delegate some of the responsibilities to capable individuals, allowing Moses to focus on the most critical matters. This delegation not only lightened Moses' burden, but also ensured a more efficient and equitable system of governance.

Delegating tasks is not a sign of weakness or incompetence, but rather a strategic and wise decision. It acknowledges the value of shared leadership and the diverse strengths of the team. However, effective delegation requires clear communication, proper training, and ongoing support. It is essential to communicate expectations, provide resources, and offer guidance as needed to ensure success.

By delegating tasks, you empower others, foster growth, and create opportunities for individuals to flourish in their giftings. It enables the ministry to operate more efficiently, as responsibilities are distributed among capable team members. Ultimately, delegation cultivates a culture of collaboration, trust, and shared responsibility, advancing the mission of the children's ministry and allowing it to thrive.

THE THREE S'S.

The importance of systems, structure, and spirituality is critical when it comes to organizational growth, including children's ministry. These three elements work together to provide a solid foundation, promote efficiency, and create a healthy spiritual environment within the ministry. The story of Nehemiah in the Old Testament provides a great example of how these elements can contribute to organizational growth.

First, Nehemiah demonstrated the significance of systems by meticulously planning and organizing the task of rebuilding the walls of Jerusalem. He assessed the situation, devised a strategic plan, and assigned responsibilities to different groups of people (Nehemiah 2:11-18). This systematic approach ensured that the work progressed smoothly and efficiently, leading to the successful completion of the project.

Second, Nehemiah emphasized the importance of structure in his leadership. He appointed leaders, established clear roles and responsibilities, and developed a sense of accountability among the people (Nehemiah 3:1-32). This structure provided a framework for collaboration and coordination, enabling the collective effort to achieve the desired outcome.

Lastly, Nehemiah understood the spiritual dimension of organizational growth. He prioritized prayer, seeking God's guidance, and leading the people in a spiritual revival (Nehemiah 1:4-11; Nehemiah 9:1-3). He recognized that true growth and success come from a deep reliance on God's wisdom, strength, and guidance. Nehemiah's spiritual leadership created an environment where the people's hearts were aligned with God's purposes, resulting in not just physical restoration, but also spiritual renewal.

In children's ministry, adopting systems and structure helps to streamline processes, ensure clarity of roles, and maximize efficiency. This includes establishing clear volunteer onboarding procedures, curriculum planning and implementation, and effective communication channels. Simultaneously, maintaining a strong spiritual foundation is vital. Prayer, seeking God's direction, and nurturing a culture of worship and spiritual growth among the team and the children they serve creates an atmosphere where God's transformative work can flourish.

When systems, structure, and spirituality are integrated; children's ministries can experience growth that goes beyond mere organizational expansion. It becomes a place where lives are impacted, children encounter God's love, and families are strengthened. Nehemiah's example reminds us of the power and effectiveness of these elements in building and growing a ministry that honors God and blesses the community it serves.

AVOIDING BURNOUT.

Avoiding burnout requires intentional self-care, healthy boundaries, and a reliance on God's strength. The following principles, supported by relevant Bible verses, can guide us in navigating this important aspect of our lives.

First, prioritize regular rest and Sabbath. In Mark 6:31, Jesus tells his disciples, "Come with me by yourselves to a quiet place and get some rest." Just as Jesus recognized the need for rest, we must make space for rejuvenation and replenishment. Establishing regular times of rest, setting aside moments for self-care, and embracing Sabbath principles can help prevent burnout and foster spiritual and emotional renewal.

Second, seek support and accountability. In Ecclesiastes 4:9-10, the importance of companionship and mutual support is emphasized: "Two are better than one because they have a good return for their labor. If either of them falls down, one can help the other up." Surrounding yourself with a network of trusted individuals who can provide encouragement, prayer, and wise counsel is vital for navigating challenges and avoiding burnout.

Furthermore, practice healthy boundaries. Jesus Himself exemplified this principle by withdrawing to solitary places to pray (Luke 5:16). Setting boundaries around work hours, personal time, and ministry responsibilities helps create a healthy balance and prevents overextension. Learning to say "no" when necessary and delegating tasks to capable individuals can also alleviate the burden of excessive workload.

Lastly, cultivate a vibrant and intimate relationship with God. In Isaiah 40:31, it says, "But those who hope in the LORD will renew their strength. They will soar on wings like eagles; they will run and not grow weary, they will walk and not be faint." Regularly spending time in prayer, studying Scripture, and seeking God's presence nourishes the spirit and provides the strength and guidance needed to avoid burnout.

By integrating these principles into your life, you can safeguard yourself against burnout, ensuring that your ministry remains fruitful, sustainable, and infused with joy. Remembering Jesus' invitation to find rest in Him (Matthew 11:28-30) and embracing his grace, you can navigate the demands of ministry while preserving your own well-being and effectively serving others.

DON'T LOSE HEART.

Men serving in children's ministry face unique challenges and may encounter discouragement along their journey. It is essential to stay focused on your calling and recommit yourself to the work you have been entrusted with. When doubts and questions arise from others, it's important not to let those voices deter you from your path.

There were times when people questioned my calling to children's ministry, wondering why I wasn't pursuing opportunities with adults or seeking my own church. But I knew deep in my heart that God had called me to serve the children and families, to invest in their lives and help shape their faith. Their questions and doubts couldn't overshadow the calling I had received.

As men in children's ministry, it is crucial to recommit ourselves to God's calling on our lives. We must remind ourselves that our ultimate audience is the Lord, and it is his approval we seek. Hebrews 12:2 reminds us to "fix our eyes on Jesus, the pioneer and perfecter of faith." When we keep our focus on Him, we are able to overcome discouragement and stay true to our calling.

Recommitting to our calling means surrendering ourselves to God daily, seeking his guidance, strength, and wisdom. It involves aligning our hearts and minds with his purposes, remembering that we serve Him first and foremost. Galatians 6:9 encourages us, "Let us not become weary in doing good, for at the proper time we will reap a harvest if we do not give up." The work we do in children's ministry has an eternal impact, and we must persevere in the face of challenges.

Don't allow the opinions or expectations of others to distract you from the path God has set before you. Stay committed, knowing that your obedience to his calling brings Him glory and transforms lives. Seek support from like-minded individuals who understand the unique challenges and joys of children's ministry. Surround yourself with a community of believers who can encourage, uplift, and pray for you.

Recommit to God daily, asking Him for the strength and courage to continue serving faithfully. Trust that He will equip you for every task and provide the necessary resources and support along the way. Your commitment to children's ministry matters, and God will use your faithful service to impact countless lives for his kingdom. Stay steadfast, focused on the Lord, and let his approval be your guiding force.

CLOSING THOUGHTS.

In closing, I want to address each one of you men who have dedicated yourselves to serving in children's ministry. You are truly making a difference in the lives of kids and families, and I want to encourage you to keep pressing forward, even when the road gets tough. In this journey, there may be moments when you feel discouraged, when you question your impact, or when you grow weary. But I urge you to not lose heart.

Remember, you are not alone in this calling. Stay connected to a community of believers who can provide support, encouragement, and accountability. Surround yourself with like-minded people who understand the unique challenges and joys of children's ministry. Lean on one another, share your triumphs and struggles, and learn from each other's experiences. Together, you can lift each other up and continue to grow in your ministry effectiveness.

Furthermore, lean into your calling with renewed fervor. Recognize that God has entrusted you with the task of nurturing the faith of the next generation. Embrace this responsibility wholeheartedly, knowing that your efforts have eternal significance. Your role as a leader in children's ministry is invaluable, and your impact will extend far beyond what you can comprehend.

Embrace a growth mindset, always seeking to improve and develop as a leader. Be open to new ideas, innovative approaches, and continuous learning. Stay informed about current trends, research, and resources that can enhance your ministry. Never settle for complacency, but rather strive to reach new heights in your effectiveness and impact.

Amidst the demands of ministry, do not neglect your own well-being. Take care of yourself physically, emotionally, and spiritually. Prioritize self-care, ensuring that you have the energy, mental clarity, and spiritual strength to pour into the lives of others. Take time for rest, relaxation, and rejuvenation. Nurture your relationship with God, seeking his guidance, strength, and wisdom as you navigate the joys and challenges of children's ministry.

Lastly, I invite you to recommit yourself to serving in children's ministry until the Lord leads you elsewhere. Remain steadfast in your dedication to shaping the lives of young ones. Your commitment, passion, and perseverance are invaluable in this vital ministry.

Thank you for answering the call to serve in children's ministry. Your love, care, and investment in the lives of children will have a lasting impact for generations to come. May you continue to walk boldly in your calling, knowing that God is with you every step of the way. Keep serving with all your heart, and may the Lord bless your efforts abundantly. I believe in you!

ACKNOWLEDGEMENT

I want to express my heartfelt gratitude to all the incredible men and women serving in children's ministry every week. This book may be short, but its message is undeniably important. Your dedication and passion in ministering to kids inspire me, and I am thankful for the impact you are making in their lives. What you do matters, and your investment in the lives of kids will leave a lasting legacy for God's Kingdom. Keep shining brightly as KidMEN, and may you continue to make a profound difference in the lives of young ones everywhere!

SHARE THIS MANIFESTO

Who else needs to read this book? Make a list of men on your team or at other churches in your community who need to read it and then circulate the book when you're done. Add a few names, then pass it on (cross yourself off the list before you do.)

_____

_____

_____

_____

_____

_____

_____

Please return this to: _____

IF YOU'VE ENJOYED
KIDMEN:
A MANIFESTO FOR
MEN SERVING IN CHILDREN'S MINISTRY

check out these other thought-provoking and inspiring books
by Ryan Frank.

Friends In Real Life

Eat the Frog First

Ten Sentences to Revolutionize Your Ministry

The Volunteer Code

Give Me Jesus

9 Things They Didn't Teach Me in College About Children's Ministry

**Visit www.RyanFrank.com for more information…
and to find all of his social links.**

Printed in the USA
CPSIA information can be obtained
at www.ICGtesting.com
JSHW050551180823
46593JS00004B/16